I0752947

Blueberry Moon

By Heather Van Dam

Illustrated by Alahna Roach

Blueberry Moon

ISBN 978-1-943424-36-8
Library of Congress Control Number: 2018946490

A portion of the profits from this book will be donated to the important work of Maine Coast Heritage Trust

North Country Press
Unity, Maine

Table of Contents

Preface

Blueberry Moon is a compilation of Haiku, a traditional form of Japanese poetry, and answering ink paintings. The Haiku totals 17 syllables which consists of 3 lines and rarely rhymes. The first and last lines of a Haiku have 5 syllables while the middle line has 7 syllables. In this small amount of space observations of nature are usually described without extended fanfare. The Haiku started in Japanese literature during the 17th century. After World War II, the Haiku was written and shared in multiple languages.

The ink paintings in Blueberry Moon are inspired by Sumi-e, a Japanese art of painting using black ink created by rubbing an ink stick against a wet stone. Once a stroke is painted, it cannot be erased, making it a technically demanding art form. The goal of ink painting is not to create a visual likeness, but to capture the essence of the subject, usually an object or scene in the natural world. Fluid, but frugal, mark making is the respected form through which so much richness is conveyed. In true Sumi-e painting all manner of marks are made with a bamboo brush, but for the illustrations in this book, the artist took creative liberty and used a bamboo ink pen to add lines over the brushwork. Most ink paintings are composed using only black ink or occasionally colored ink; this book departed from the Japanese form to add watercolor and chalk pastel.

East Asian painting is historically referred to as "writing a painting" and "painting a poem." We drew upon the haiku and ink painting traditions to express those small moments when nature's beauty delights and connects us to the present.

Acknowledgements

This work would not have been possible to share without the support of Patricia Newell, thank you for taking a chance with our first book of haiku poems and ink paintings. We appreciate every email, phone call and skype date.

We are grateful to Jess LeClair whose critical eye and skill as a Graphic Designer brought this vision to fruition. And for your magical business: www.AdventureAwaitsME.com

To our dear friend, Marilyn Ortega, thank you.

From Heather:

I would like to extend thanks to my long-term writing partner, Teyonda Hall, for the many ocean walks and countless writing dates, we are in this word play for life! To Leslie Conner, thank-you for stocking me up with years of *Writer's Digest* magazine. To Christi Gibbs, for your many supportive phone calls to promote this book before it was even written. To my amazing parents, Edgar & Constance, for always supporting & believing in every dream I pursue and to my sisters, who are the yin to my yang and vice versa.

Last, but never least, to my husband, Seth, who admits he does not "get" poetry, yet listens to all of mine; for being my biggest fan and my safe confidant.

From Alahna:

Deep gratitude goes to my four sons for the present-centered wisdom and attention they bring to each moment and to my fiancé, Tom, for his humor, his integrity in striving for an equitable world and for his constant, unwavering support. To my parents and sister, for their joyful, loving upbringing and for the home they created; full of loud singing, creative freedom and a compassionate, rich emotional life. To my cousin, Brian Watson, for sharing wisdom long ago about God's secret names, *Yes* and *Now,* and for his encouragement to honor the inspiration of Japanese art forms with my own humble offerings.

And finally, to all of the living things in this book and the world, who coexist in balance and connect us with ourselves and one another.

Dedicated with love to our beautiful Mothers

Constance Van Dam

&

Ann Roach

the tea is ready
trees dapple scattered patterns
wisps of steam disperse

unfurl vibrantly
growing green in springtime dream
daffodil peeking

fluorescent green shoots
through melting granular snow
mud intermingles

fast moving storm clouds
heavy rains soak new gardens
robins flit through fog

delicate blossoms
profusion of perfume brief
apple groves' pink dress

darting from tree top
red wings aloft he warbles
cardinals mate for life

cool breeze growing leaves
bright green rustling fluttering
birds ascend skyward

breeze through poplar trees
sea roses fragrant heaven
scattered seaweed shore

deep in the gray mist
beyond is invisible
above, the seagulls

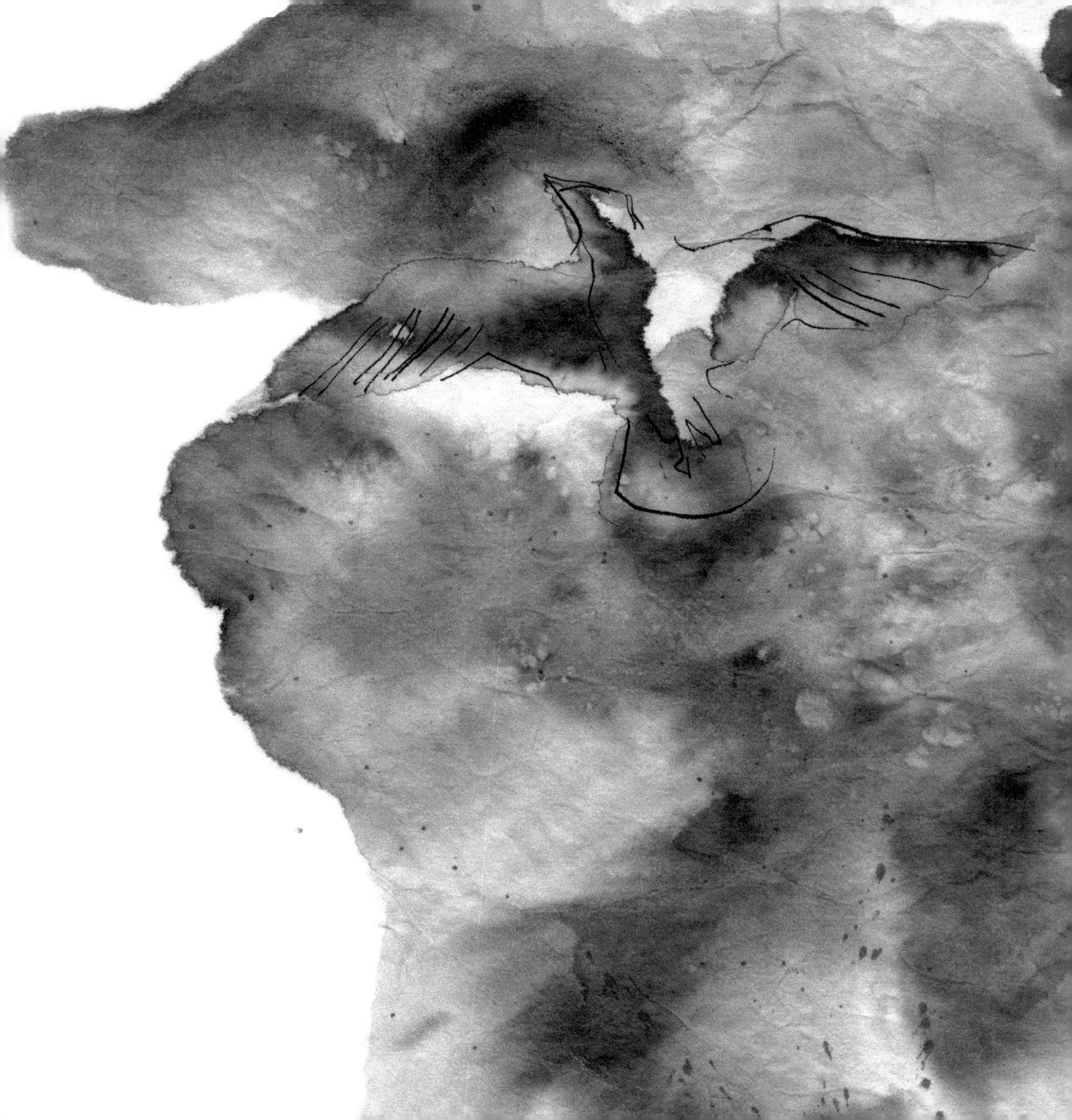

fishing boats anchored
orange buoys bobbing calm
gentle midday tide

in the clear blue sky
waves crashing softening rocks
a limitless view

sinking into blue
minnows hiding in seaweed
to the surface sun

edges of day sink
twilight bugs create ripples
a regal loon wails

big eyed dragonflies
Grandma's red geraniums
four gossamer wings

venerable pallor
damp green moss dresses bare trees
knotted bark texture

weathered picnic bench
rusty nails push splintered wood
ants march unhurried

walking in the rain
thunder bright flashes dear friend
baptized by nature

a rocky inlet
water tugging the shoreline
endless rivulets

weathered rocks by shore
aqua, navy, sky blue waves
tiptoeing children

rippling dark blue waves
lone seagull above silent
afternoon sun shade

sweet holy breathing
misty oceanside matching
endless forever

seals bask unperturbed
ocean waves crashing downward
on rocky outcrops

seagull belly full
broken bits of shell awash
cream colored spilling

seeded brown middle
bees swoon drunken yellow dust
tall stemmed sunflower

to be August rain
welcome droplets earth refreshed
tired leaves revive

late afternoon sun
forest particles floating
light streams through tall birch

lowbush horizon
bucket tipped makeshift lunch break
sun warmed blueberries

silent cicadas
squirrels scamper limb to limb
sunken apples drop

autumn wraps warmly
pumpkins steal garden spaces
yellow leaves curl in

cold wind rushing through
acres of blueberry fields
November stillness

evening winds whisper
half-moon glows like candlelight
forest shadows wave

in the twilight hour
the gathering mist and chill
autumn goes to sleep

crinkled dry brown leaf
clinging to the stable tree
rustling the year end

last year's leaves peeking
brown memories through the snow
crunching the deer pass

snowflakes twirling down
heartbeats solitary sound
quiet winter day

empty beach mornings
whipping frozen ice pellets
waves in a temper

the trees are empty
heavy snow curls branches down
hibernation sleep

morning earlier
low slung clouds manifest snow
tick tock winter clock

the horizon dark
void of sound the forest sleeps
stars the soul of night

ABOUT THE AUTHOR AND ARTIST

Heather holds an MA in Rural Community Studies from Goddard College and a bachelor's degree in Sociology from the University of Southern Maine. When Heather is not writing or outdoors, you can find her educating about the benefits of Ayurvedic wellness and teaching various fitness classes. She currently resides in Richmond, Virginia with her husband, Seth and a small jungle of indoor plants.

Alahna is currently applying her MA in Transpersonal Counseling and Art Therapy to her mothering of four creative and dreamy sons, as well as her volunteer work in her beloved hometown community of Down East, Maine. She lives most seasons in a stand of birch trees on the coast with her beloved, Tom, and their boys; they summer amongst the pines in Western Maine, near the Kawanhee Inn.

Alahna and Heather met at a church picnic many years ago, as children roaming wild and free beside the ocean in Down East Maine. In their many adventures since, their love of the natural world has continued to unite them, even as distance separates. The poems in this book, and their answering paintings, represent an intimate conversation between two old friends about the tender and tangible beauty of their roots.

www.ingramcontent.com/pod-product-compliance
Lightning Source LLC
LaVergne TN
LVHW070919120826
845154LV00019BB/25
* 9 7 8 1 9 4 3 4 2 4 3 6 8 *